THE CREATION OF

THE INCREDIBLE HULK®

ERIC FEIN

The Rosen Publishing Group, Inc.,
New York

For my family

Published in 2007 by The Rosen Publishing Group, Inc.
29 East 21st Street, New York, NY 10010

First Edition

Thanks to Marvel Entertainment, Inc.: Avi Arad, James Hinton, Mary Law, Bruno Maglione, Tim Rothwell, Mickey Stern, Alberta Stewart, and Carl Suecoff

Library of Congress Cataloging-in-Publication Data

Fein, Eric.
The creation of the Incredible Hulk/Eric Fein.
    p. cm.—(Action Heroes)
Includes bibliographical references and index.
ISBN 1-4042-0764-3 (library binding)
1. Hulk (Comic strip)
I. Title. II. Series.
PN6728.H8F45 2007
741.5'973—dc22

2005035267

Manufactured in the United States of America

On the cover: The Incredible Hulk.

CONTENTS

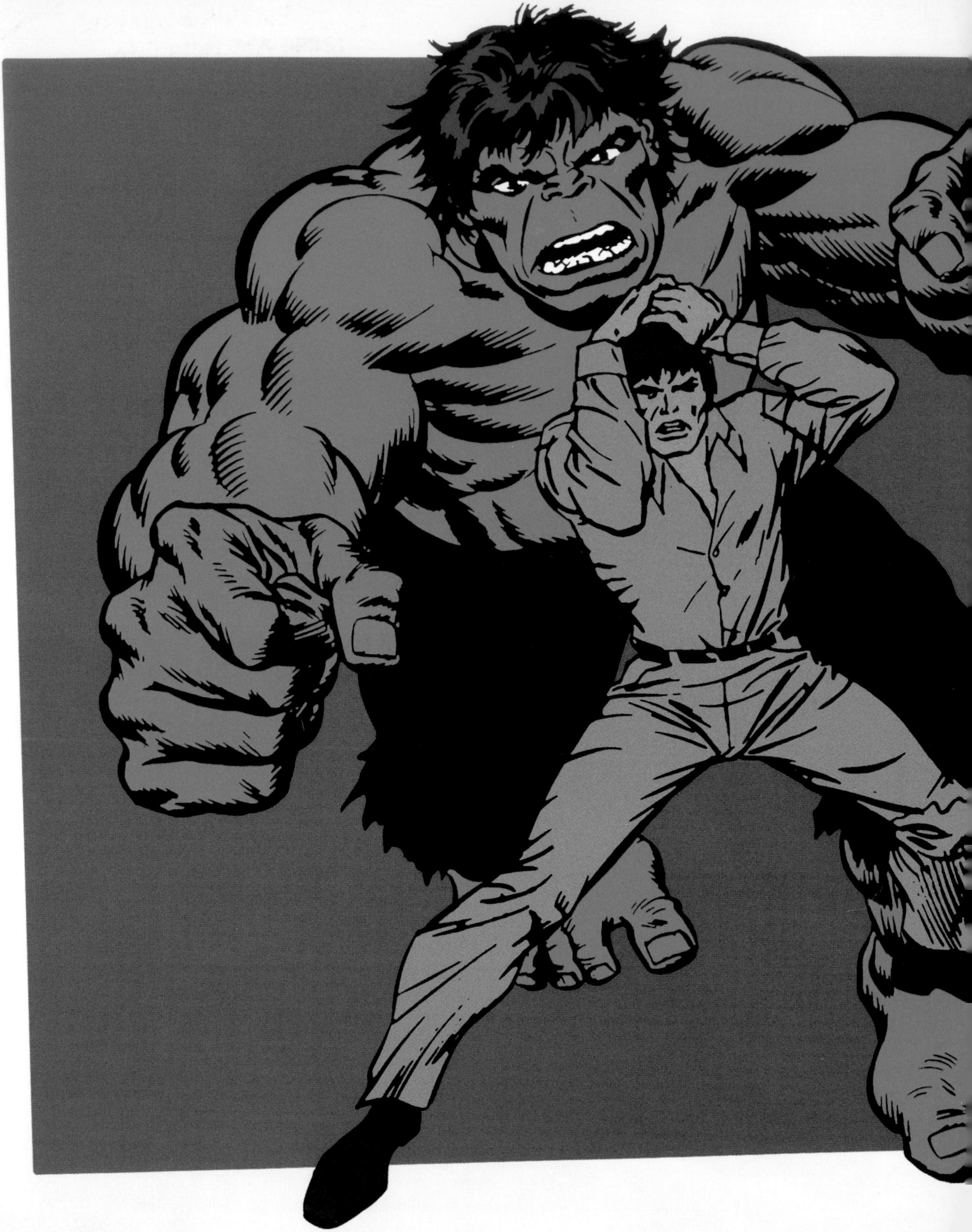

INTRODUCTION

In 1961, Stan Lee and Jack Kirby started what is known as the Marvel age of comics when they created the Fantastic Four—a team of Super Heroes who were unlike any others seen up until that time. Lee was the writer, and Kirby was the artist.

The Fantastic Four was a close-knit group of friends and family who accidentally came about their superpowers. They did not always act like Super Heroes. In fact, they did not necessarily like being heroes, and they often argued with each other. When the book came out, it was an instant success. Comic book fans then demanded more heroes like the Fantastic Four, and Stan and Jack felt obliged to give the fans what they wanted. Next, instead of co-creating another team of heroes, they decided to focus on one hero. He would be huge, superstrong, and ultimately more monster than hero. He would be much more like the Fantastic Four's Thing, Ben Grimm. Stan named this new hero the Incredible Hulk.

The Incredible Hulk was scientist Bruce Banner. Banner worked for the U.S. military at a secret base in New Mexico, where he created a powerful new weapon called a gamma bomb. However, just before the bomb was set to be tested, a teenager named Rick Jones snuck onto the test site. Banner left the safety of his lab to rescue the teen, and he got caught in the gamma bomb's blast. The radiation from it turned him into the Incredible Hulk.

Banner's transformations into the Hulk are triggered by emotions such as anger, fear, or excitement. The Hulk is chased around the country by those who want to destroy him, including the military. The Hulk is an outsider who is feared and distrusted by both regular people and other Super Heroes. Indeed, the Hulk is one of comic books' greatest tragic figures. He is a character who is lonely and at times scared. However, he is unable to accept the help of others. He is forever destined to be an outsider from the rest of humanity.

1 THE SECRET ORIGINS OF STAN AND JACK

Stan Lee and Jack Kirby have secret identities. Stan was born Stanley Martin Lieber. Jack's birth name is Jacob Kurtzberg. Both men changed their names when they entered the comic book industry, as was common practice in its early stages. The two came from very similar backgrounds, and they were destined to meet and make comic book history.

Jack Kirby was born on August 28, 1917, to Benjamin and Rosemary Kurtzberg. He was raised on the Lower East Side of Manhattan in New York City. Jack had a younger brother named David. His father, Benjamin, worked in the clothing business, and his mother, Rosemary, worked in a bakery and as a seamstress to help support the family.

Stan Lee was born in New York City on December 28, 1922, to Jack and Celia Lieber, who were Romanian immigrants.

This photograph is of Jack Kirby with his parents, Benjamin and Rosemary. Jack originally wanted a career in Hollywood movies. However, his mother refused to let him move to California.

Stan also had a younger brother, Larry, who was born when Stan was about nine years old. The family was very poor. Stan's father worked as a dress cutter in Manhattan, but when the Great Depression (1929–1939) hit, he found it very difficult to find steady work.

ESCAPING INTO FANTASY

Stan and Jack also had a few interests in common when they were growing up. They both loved to read and watch movies. These interests would benefit them years later when they co-created the Incredible Hulk. Books and movies allowed the two boys to escape the harsh realities of their daily lives for a few hours. Stan did his own illustrated stories to amuse himself and to forget his troubles.

Stan enjoyed reading the works of many different writers. Some of his favorite authors were H. G. Wells, Mark Twain, and William Shakespeare. As for movies, Stan loved all kinds: comedy, drama, adventure, and horror. Some of his favorites are *Gunga Din* (1939), the films of Charlie Chaplin, *Frankenstein* (1931), and *King Kong* (1933).

Jack Kirby became hooked on pulp magazines as a young boy. He loved their covers, which looked like movie posters and featured eye-catching images. This was especially true for science fiction and horror pulps. Their covers usually featured monsters, space aliens, and rocket ships. Jack also enjoyed reading the comic strips published in newspapers, particularly *Prince Valiant* by artist Hal Foster. Jack also liked the work of Milton Canniff and other artists. He taught himself how to draw by studying his favorite comic strips. By the time he was nineteen, Jack was getting professional work drawing comic strips and pictures for newspaper editorials.

MAKING COMICS

Lee and Kirby entered the comic book industry while it was in its early stages in the mid- to late 1930s. During this period, comic books were shifting away from being collected reprints of comic strips originally printed in newspapers. In 1938, the first comic book Super Hero was introduced. The comic book was *Action Comics* #1, published by DC Comics. The Super Hero it featured was Superman. He was the first comic book Super Hero and the inspiration for many of the Super Heroes that followed his introduction. Other comic book publishers started to publish their own versions of Superman.

Martin Goodman was one such publisher. His company, Timely Publications, started as a publisher of pulp magazines, such as *Mystery Tales* and *Gunsmoke Western*. Goodman's publishing philosophy was to copy whatever was selling well at the time. When

Super Hero comic books became hot, he started a comic book company and named it Timely Comics. However, over the years it would be known by several different names. Finally, in the early 1960s, the company was officially named Marvel Comics.

The success of *Marvel Comics* #1 in 1939 sparked Goodman to rush out more comic books. He hired writer and artist Joe Simon to be in charge of his comic book line. Goodman knew of Simon from his work at Funnies, Inc., the company that created the stories that Goodman bought to use in his comic books. Simon had met Kirby while working for another comic book publisher. The two decided to become partners. Simon and Kirby then went to work for Goodman and co-created Captain America in 1941. When the first issue hit the newsstands, it was an immediate success. The team was so busy that they immediately needed additional help. A notice then went out for an office assistant.

THE OFFICE BOY WONDER

Goodman was married to Stan Lee's cousin Jean, making them cousins-in-law. When Lee found out through a family member that

Marvel Comics #1 is one of the most valuable comic books ever published. Back in 1939, it sold for 10 cents. Today, a copy in near mint, or perfect, condition is worth more than $175,000! The cover to *Marvel Comics* #1 was originally going to spotlight the Sub-Mariner. Sub-Mariner artist Bill Everett even did a rough color version of it. However, for reasons lost to history, Martin Goodman decided to go with the Human Torch on the cover instead.

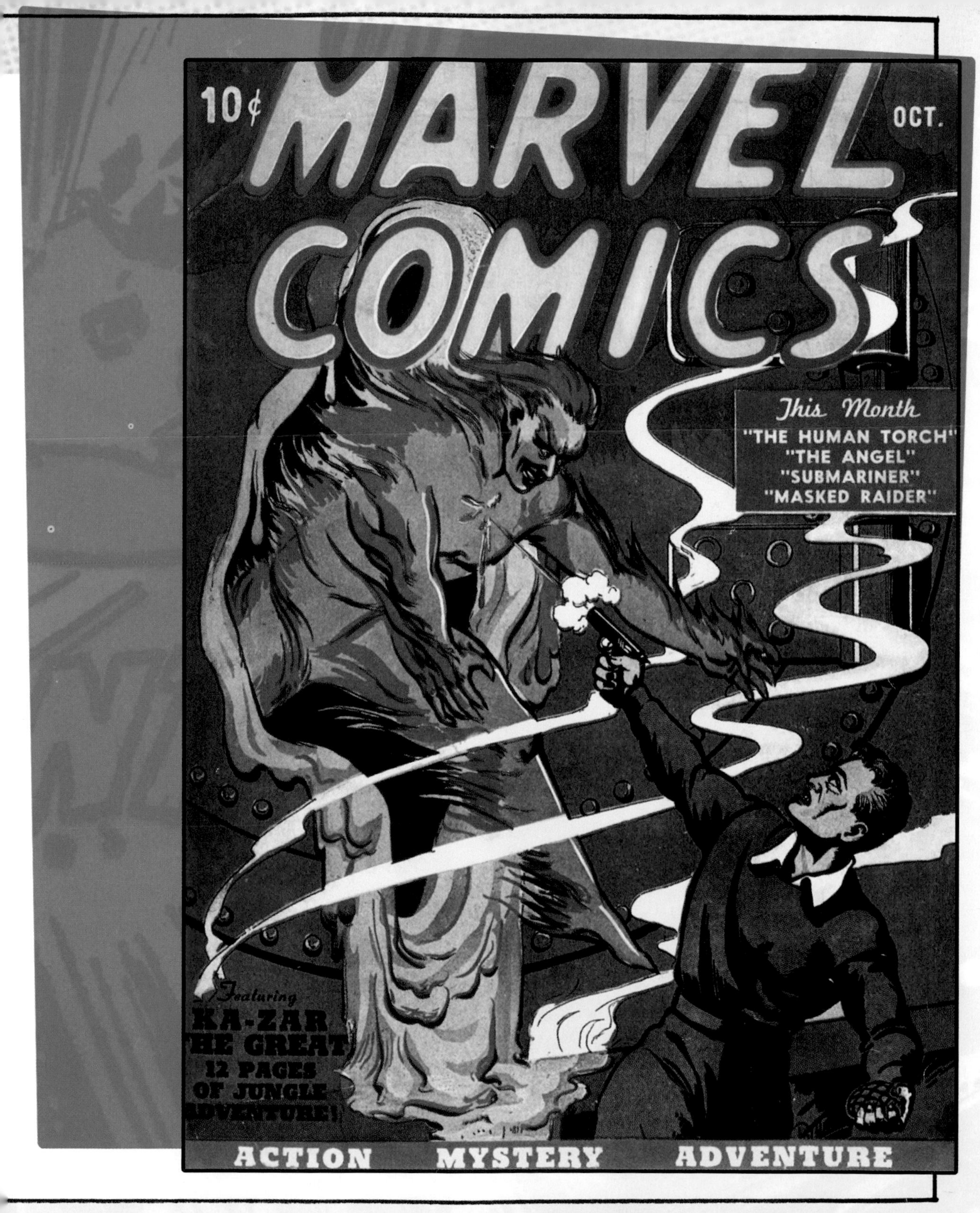
10¢
MARVEL COMICS
OCT.
This Month
"THE HUMAN TORCH"
"THE ANGEL"
"SUBMARINER"
"MASKED RAIDER"
Featuring
KA-ZAR THE GREAT
12 PAGES OF JUNGLE ADVENTURE!
ACTION MYSTERY ADVENTURE

there was a job available at Goodman's company, he immediately applied and got the job. However, Lee had not been well acquainted with Goodman up to that point. When he started working at Marvel in late 1940, Lee was seventeen years old. He had only recently graduated from high school. In Les Daniels's *Marvel: Five Fabulous Decades of the World's Greatest Comics*, published in 1991, Lee recounted his early days at Marvel, saying, "I did proofreading, I'd run errands, I'd erase the penciling from the inked pages, but then very quickly they let me do writing and I got into it."

At the end of 1941, Simon and Kirby had a disagreement with Goodman over business matters and quit the company. Goodman then put eighteen-year-old Lee in charge of Marvel. As editor, Lee was responsible for hiring and working with the writers, pencillers, inkers, colorists, and letterers and making sure the books got to the printer on time.

MARVEL COMICS #1

Martin Goodman's first comic book was *Marvel Comics* #1 (1939). It would go on to become one of the most important comic books ever published. First, it featured the debuts of two characters that would have major roles throughout Marvel's history: Prince Namor, the Sub-Mariner, and the Human Torch. Artist Bill Everett co-created Namor. The Human Torch was co-created by Carl Burgos. Burgos worked off and on at Marvel over the years doing many different comic books in addition to the Human Torch. In the early 1960s, Everett co-created the superhero Daredevil with Stan Lee. He also inked several Hulk stories that appeared in *Tales to Astonish*.

BIG CHANGES IN THE COMIC BOOK INDUSTRY

Both Lee and Kirby served in World War II (1939–1945). After they served in the war, they returned to work in the comic book field, yet superhero comics were no longer as popular as they once were. There were many reasons for this. Soldiers had been a large part of the audience during the war, but now they were not as interested in comic books. They were getting married, going to school, or going to work. Also, with restrictions on paper use lifted, more publishers began putting out more superhero comic books. Suddenly, there was more product than demand. Publishers started to experiment with different, non-superhero types of comic books. They introduced crime comic books, horror comic books, and even western comic books.

Kirby reteamed with Simon and co-created *Young Romance* in 1947. It was the first romance comic ever published, and it became a big hit. Romance comic books attracted people, especially women, who were not interested in superheroes.

When Lee returned to Marvel, he found that the company was now focusing on all sorts of comic books, including westerns, war stories, and horror. When Goodman saw how well romance comics were selling, he had Lee create those, too.

THE HORROR OF IT ALL!

The 1950s were not a kind decade to comic books. A handful of experts on child behavior felt that comic books were the cause of juvenile delinquency and even crime. These wild claims led the U.S. Congress to hold hearings on the matter. The bad publicity hurt sales, and many of the smaller companies went out of business. Because of the poor sales, Marvel did not produce as many books. As a result, Lee was forced to fire most of the staff.

In the mid-1950s, Kirby ended his partnership with Simon. Kirby went to work for DC Comics. After a few years, he left there and returned to Marvel. It was good timing because Lee needed an artist to draw monster stories. This would be the first time the two worked together as writer and artist. They honed their storytelling skills on numerous monster stories. This gave them the experience they needed when they co-created the Incredible Hulk a few years later.

2 THE MARVEL AGE OF COMICS

As the 1960s began, the United States was undergoing major changes as it dealt with problems at home and abroad. America was trying to prevent the spread of Communism, led by the Soviet Union, around the world. This conflict between the two superpowers came to be known as the Cold War (1945–1991). Both countries had nuclear weapons that could annihilate one another as well as devastate the earth. The threat of nuclear war between the two superpowers hung over the world.

Both countries were also trying to gain control of outer space. In the late 1950s, the Soviets successfully launched several spacecraft into outer space. The United States created the space agency NASA. In 1961, NASA successfully sent the first man into space.

At home, Americans were confronted by the ugly reality of racism in the country. The civil rights movement (mid-1950s to mid-1960s) took hold during this time. Across the country, people began to protest for equal rights for all Americans. Also at this time, young people began to question the government. They were upset with the country's involvement in the southeastern Asian country of Vietnam. Many young men refused to be drafted and fight in the Vietnam War (1957–1975). These problems divided the country, and the mass

SUPER HEROES THE DC COMICS WAY

Only a handful of Super Hero comics continued to be published in the early 1960s. DC Comics published most of these and was home to some of the most popular heroes of all time: Superman, Batman, and Wonder Woman. Before Lee and Kirby started co-creating Super Hero comics in 1961, Super Heroes were all very similar in their behavior and attitude. They were all handsome and well mannered, and few if any had troubles in their private lives. They accepted their fate to be Super Heroes with grace. These Super Heroes were not concerned with living normal lives or how their powers would affect their loved ones. The DC Comics Super Heroes lived in fictional cities that were not in the real world. Superman lived in Metropolis. Batman lived in Gotham City.

Around 1960, DC Comics teamed Superman, Batman, and Wonder Woman with some newer versions of the Flash, Green Lantern, Aquaman, and the Martian Manhunter. They called this new super team the Justice League of America (or JLA). Because the book featured different Super Heroes, it attracted fans of each hero, and this helped to make it a best-selling series. Of course, when Goodman found out about it, he ordered Lee to co-create a Marvel version of the book.

media reflected them in such movies as *Dr. Strangelove* and *Guess Who's Coming to Dinner?* as well as in books such as *Catch-22* and *One Flew Over the Cuckoo's Nest.* However, comic books were slow to show this unrest on their pages.

FANTASTIC BEGINNINGS

By 1961, Lee had reached a point in his life where he was ready to quit comics. He was unhappy with the lack of creative freedom he had at Marvel. Goodman felt that comic book stories should be simple and

This cover of *Fantastic Four* #3 shows the team in costumes for the first time. Lee and Kirby are at their best here: Kirby's layout is simple yet bold. Lee wrote cover text that was informative but fun.

straightforward and not use big words or challenging concepts. Lee did not think that comics would survive for much longer. When Goodman asked him to create a Super Hero group to compete with the DC Comics' Justice League of America, Lee wanted to refuse. However, Lee's wife, Joan, convinced him to take a shot at the project, urging him to co-create the book the way he thought it should be done.

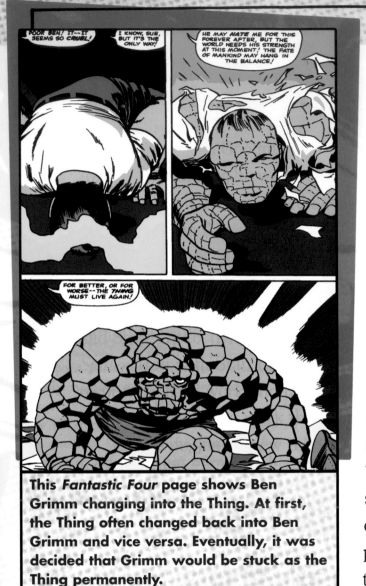

Speech bubbles: POOR BEN! IT--IT SEEMS SO CRUEL!

I KNOW, SUE, BUT IT'S THE ONLY WAY!

HE MAY HATE ME FOR THIS FOREVER AFTER, BUT THE WORLD NEEDS HIS STRENGTH AT THIS MOMENT! THE FATE OF MANKIND MAY HANG IN THE BALANCE!

FOR BETTER, OR FOR WORSE--THE THING MUST LIVE AGAIN!

This *Fantastic Four* page shows Ben Grimm changing into the Thing. At first, the Thing often changed back into Ben Grimm and vice versa. Eventually, it was decided that Grimm would be stuck as the Thing permanently.

That way, if the book flopped and he was fired, at least he had done it his way.

Lee then came up with the basic idea for what would become the Fantastic Four and discussed it with Kirby. Kirby took Lee's basic story idea and fleshed it out into a twenty-five-page story. Lee had developed a method of working during his years as an editor. He would give the artist a plot instead of a full script. The artist would draw the story, adding scenes of his own. Then, Lee would take the pages and add the dialogue in the form of word balloons and captions. This way of working came to be known as the Marvel method. The method used by most other comic book companies involved the writer writing a full script that had the dialogue as well as the captions included with the art notes to the artist.

Lee's Fantastic Four stories were more character-driven than the superhero stories published by other companies at that time. Lee was more interested in learning about the characters—what they believed in, what they were afraid of—rather than what kind of deathtrap they had to escape from. He also believed that it was important for the characters to live in real places. In the first issue of *Fantastic Four*, the team lived in Central City, but in the very next issue, that was changed to New York City. Lee wanted the readers to feel that the Marvel characters lived in the world just outside their windows.

Lee and Kirby did another thing that had never been done by co-creating stories that continued on for more than one issue. Most comic books had stories that were self-contained and did not make mention of events happening in other books in the same comic book line. Lee decided that the Marvel books would all take place in one fictional universe and that events that happened in one book would be referenced in another, an attention to detail and consistency that is known as continuity.

FAN REACTIONS

Comic book readers went crazy for *Fantastic Four*. Fan mail started to arrive at the office within a week or so of *Fantastic Four* #1 going on sale. Up until that time, this kind of reader response was a rarity in the comic book world. Upon reading the letters, Lee saw that the Thing was the favorite character of most of the fans. He then decided that the next Super Hero book Marvel published would focus on a hero that looked and acted like a monster.

3 AN INCREDIBLE CREATION

In creating a Super Hero similar to the Thing, Lee remembered back to the Frankenstein movie he had seen as a child. In *Origins of Marvel Comics*, published in 1974, Lee described his view of Frankenstein's monster, saying, "No one could ever convince me that he was the bad guy, the villain, or the menace. It was he who was sinned against by those who feared him, by those whose first instinct was to strike out blindly at whatever they couldn't comprehend."

CREATING THE INCREDIBLE HULK

Lee took this idea of the Frankenstein monster and modernized it. The scientist would become the monster due to an experiment gone wrong. Lee also borrowed from Robert Louis Stevenson's 1886 novel *The Strange Case of Dr. Jekyll and Mr. Hyde*. In that story, a scientist drinks a potion that changes him into an anger-filled monster called Mr. Hyde. Lee's scientist would be able to change back and forth between his two identities.

Now that Lee had a basic idea of the new character, he needed the right name for it. Lee recounted how he came up with the name Hulk in his book *Excelsior!: The Amazing Life of Stan Lee*:

This is a scene from *Frankenstein* (1931). Pictured are Boris Karloff as the monster and Dwight Frye as Fritz, Dr. Frankenstein's assistant. Once in full monster costume, Karloff stood more than seven feet tall.

The name is important, because you have to convey the entire essence of your concept in a word or two. I wanted a name that conjured up an intimidating, gargantuan behemoth with a plodding brain and enormous power . . . I needed a name for this monstrous, potentially murderous, hulking brute who . . . Whoa! "Hulking brute" is the exact description, and instantly I knew "hulking" was the adjective. Well, it wasn't much of a stretch to go from "hulking" to "hulk," which sounded like the perfect noun.

Lee talked the story over with Kirby. Kirby then went off and drew the story for *The Incredible Hulk* #1.

IT'S NOT EASY BEING GREEN

The Hulk's road to comic book success was not a smooth one. In fact, the series was cancelled after only six issues. Kirby left after issue #5 to work on other Marvel projects, and Steve Ditko drew issue #6. Ditko co-created Spider-Man with Lee. During this first series, the Hulk went through many different changes. The reason for Bruce Banner transforming into the Hulk changed from issue to issue. In the first issue, the setting of the sun triggered the change. In the next issue, Banner was able to turn into the Hulk during the day. By issue #4, Banner had to use a machine that he built to turn him into the Hulk. Finally, Lee decided that extreme negative emotions (anger and fear) would be the cause of his transformations. The Hulk underwent one of his strangest changes in issue #6. When Banner changed into the Hulk, he found that he still had the head of Bruce Banner, so he had to wear a mask of the Hulk's face!

The other major change that occurred to the Hulk was his coloring. In *The Incredible Hulk* #1, Lee had the Hulk colored gray.

This is the cover of *The Incredible Hulk* #1. Today, a near mint copy is worth more than $20,000. The cover shows Bruce Banner changing into the Hulk after being exposed to gamma radiation. Since he already used cosmic rays to co-create the Fantastic Four, Stan Lee needed a different kind of radiation for the Hulk. He chose *gamma* because he liked the way it sounded.

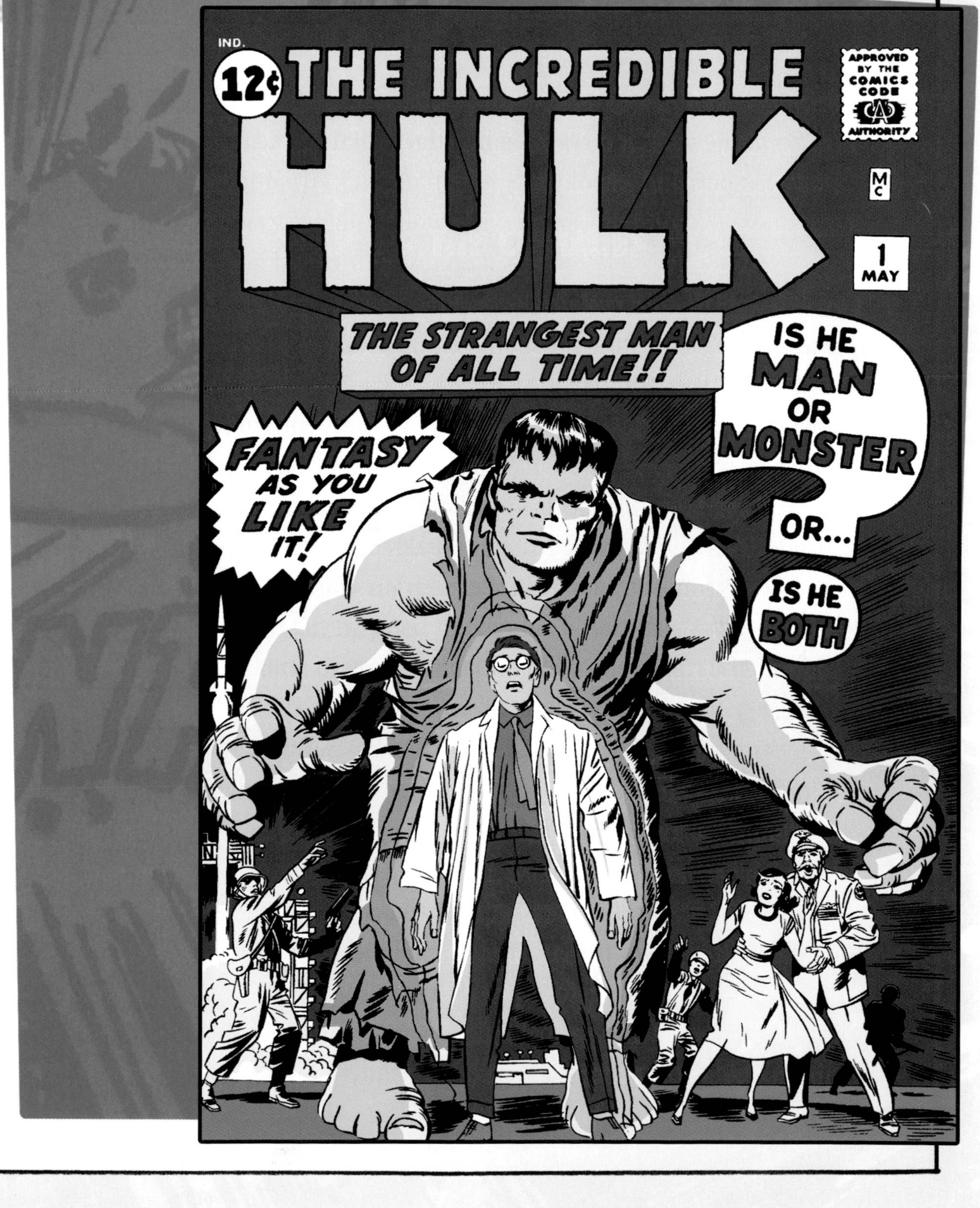

IND.
12¢
THE INCREDIBLE
HULK
APPROVED BY THE COMICS CODE AUTHORITY
MC
1
MAY
THE STRANGEST MAN OF ALL TIME!!
IS HE MAN OR MONSTER
OR...
IS HE BOTH
FANTASY AS YOU LIKE IT!

However, the printer had problems keeping to the right shade of gray. So in the second issue, Lee had the Hulk colored green, and this became his permanent color.

FRIENDS

Lee and Kirby developed a small but important supporting cast for the Hulk. Lee had never liked sidekicks. He thought no super-powered character would want to hang around with a kid. He also felt that most sidekicks, up until then, had very bland personalities and did not contribute much to the stories. Lee took his distaste for teen sidekicks and fashioned a more realistic approach in Rick Jones. Jones had an important part in the creation of the Hulk. He was the

TALES TO ASTONISH

The Hulk did not disappear from the Marvel Universe when his book was cancelled. Instead, he became a traveling menace that other Marvel heroes had to deal with. *Fantastic Four #12* featured the first fight between the Thing and the Hulk. Hulk also became a member of Marvel's new team book, *The Avengers*. However, he did not stay a member for long. In 1964, the Hulk got his own series again in another Marvel book, *Tales to Astonish*. Other Marvel writers and artists worked on the series. However, Lee and Kirby returned to the Hulk from time to time during his run in *Tales to Astonish*. This second series proved successful, and the Hulk was once again given his own series. With its 102nd issue, *Tales to Astonish* was officially re-titled *The Incredible Hulk*.

teen who had trespassed on the test site and drew Banner out into the explosion. However, Jones went from thoughtless teen to concerned friend for both Banner and the Hulk.

General Thaddeus "Thunderbolt" Ross was in charge of the Gamma Base. He was technically a good guy except when it came to Banner and the Hulk, but fans saw him only as a bad guy. Ross hated the fact that Banner, a civilian, was in charge of the gamma bomb project. Moreover, his young daughter, Betty, had a crush on Banner. When Banner became the Hulk, Ross made it his life's mission to track him down and destroy him.

This page from *The Incredible Hulk* #1 shows Banner after he has just changed back from being the Hulk. The action on the page also shows the military hunting for the Hulk as well as Betty Ross's concern for Bruce Banner.

Over the years, Bruce Banner had many different love interests. However, none were as important to him and the readers as Betty Ross. She was his true love. However, their relationship was a rocky one. It would be years before they finally found the right moment to get married. Sadly, the marriage did not have a happy ending. Betty was poisoned by one of the Hulk's enemies, the Abomination, and appeared to die.

It was later revealed that a super-secret organization saved Betty and sent her undercover to spy on the Hulk. Eventually, Bruce and Betty were reunited. Yet, once Bruce learned of her actions, he could no longer trust her, and they went their separate ways.

FOES

When Lee and Kirby co-created the Hulk, Communism was still a very real threat. Lee made the Communists the villains in several of the early Hulk stories, starting with issue #1. In that issue, Banner's assistant, Igor Starsky, turned out to be the Russian spy Igor Drenkov. It was Drenkov who was responsible for Banner's exposure to the gamma bomb because he disobeyed Banner's order to halt the countdown.

The Leader is one of the Hulk's more recognizable villains. He first appeared in *Tales to Astonish* #62. His real name was Samuel Sterns, and he was a high school dropout. He worked at a chemical factory, where he was caught in an explosion of radioactive waste. This exposure changed him by making him supersmart. More important, he changed physically. His skin became green, and the top of his skull expanded to contain his larger brain. He called himself the Leader and set up an organization to steal government secrets.

The Abomination is a Communist spy named Emil Blonsky. Blonsky wanted to learn what Banner knew about gamma radiation, so he sneaked into Banner's lab, where he accidentally triggered a machine that Banner had made to help rid himself of the Hulk. Instead, Blonsky was transformed into a hideous monster called the Abomination.

HULK WRITERS

Over the years, many of Marvel's best writers and artists have worked on the Hulk. Bill Mantlo, who wrote the book for many years, was one of the first writers to state that there was more to Banner's transformation into the Hulk than being exposed to gamma radiation. He wrote a story that showed how Banner came from an abusive home. His father was very violent, and Banner had held in all of his rage at his father for many years. Mantlo also wrote Spider-Man stories and co-created the streetwise teen crime-fighters Cloak and Dagger for Marvel.

Peter David wrote *The Incredible Hulk* from 1987 to 1998. David got his start writing a four-part story in *The Spectacular Spider-Man* that became very popular with comic book readers. He also went on to write an X-Men spin-off book, *X-Factor*.

By building on the stories written by Mantlo and others about the origins of the Hulk, Peter David helped to co-create a solid psychological foundation for Banner's transformations into the Hulk. David also was not afraid to push Banner and the Hulk in new directions. For example, he brought back the gray version of the Hulk and made him intelligent and crafty. David put him into stories in which he worked in Las Vegas as a mob enforcer. This version of the Hulk was called Joe Fixit or Mr. Fixit.

HULK ARTISTS

Over the years, the Hulk has gone through many different looks. His visual appeal to readers is just as important as his personality. Several of the best artists in comics have worked on the Hulk.

Herb Trimpe worked on *The Incredible Hulk* from 1968 to 1975 on issues 106–193. His style was very different from Kirby's. In an article published in the *Official Overstreet Comic Book Price Guide*, 34th edition (2001), Arnold T. Blumberg says, "Trimpe's Neanderthal design for the Rampaging One, with his low brow and incredibly expansive upper lip region lent a certain child-like pathos to the Hulk . . ."

In 1975, Sal Buscema took over the book and started a run that would last ten years. Many fans and professionals consider Buscema's version of the Hulk to be the definitive version of the character. Buscema was also one of the main Spider-Man artists from the 1970s through the 1990s.

Other artists, such as Todd McFarlane and John Romita Jr., have lent their talents to *The Incredible Hulk* with positive results. McFarlane went on to write and draw an ongoing Spider-Man series whose first issue sold more than two million copies. He is also one of the cofounders of Image Comics as well as the co-creator of Spawn. John Romita Jr. has penciled several high-profile Marvel series, including *The Amazing Spider-Man*, *Daredevil*, and *X-Men*.

4 HULK-A-MANIA

The Hulk touched a nerve in readers. They responded to his desire to be left alone by others, especially authority. However, when the Hulk was threatened, he would unleash his fury on those he considered his enemies and he did it without any guilt. He was a character driven by emotion, and he tapped into the readers' own personal frustrations about their lives and the world around them. Although they could not lash out at the world, the Hulk could, and it was fun to watch it happen.

MAKING COMICS FUN

Lee wanted the readers to have fun reading his stories and to feel connected to the characters as well as the co-creators. He included credits for all the people who worked on the books. Sometimes, he would

This photo shows Stan Lee *(right)* hamming it up for the cameras at the world premiere of the movie *Hulk* (2003). Joining him for the fun is the TV Hulk, Lou Ferrigno. The two had brief roles in the Hulk movie as a pair of security guards at the lab where Bruce Banner works.

give them nicknames. Kirby was usually referred to as "Jolly Jack" or "The King," while Lee called himself "Smilin' Stan" or "Stan the Man." He even gave the Hulk nicknames. He referred to the Hulk as the "jade giant" and the "green goliath" in the letters pages.

Lee loved entertaining people, and he loved playing with language. He put both to good use in co-creating a "voice" for Marvel Comics. Lee's scripting could be dramatic, humorous, or even over the top. He was not afraid to break the mood of the story by addressing the readers directly through captions and footnotes. He used the footnotes to remind readers of what happened previously in the series or to promote what was happening in another comic book. Here is an example from *The Incredible Hulk* #107 where Lee is reminding the reader that an event that a character is talking about happened last issue: "As peerlessly portrayed in our last illustrious ish!—Set It Straight Stan!"

As editor in chief, Lee was responsible for the Bullpen Bulletins and letters pages for all the books. The bullpen was the area at the Marvel office where some artists and production people worked. The bulletins gave readers an insider's view of what was going on at Marvel.

Because Lee wrote most of the books and was always rushing to meet deadlines, mistakes would happen from time to time. Instead of worrying about it, he turned it into an opportunity to have fun with the fans. Anytime a reader found a mistake in the story or art and came up with a good reason why it really wasn't a mistake, he or she would be sent a "No-Prize." The No-Prize was just an empty envelope. Printed on it was "Congratulations! This envelope contains a genuine Marvel Comics No-Prize, which you have just won!" The fans loved it.

A CHANGING RELATIONSHIP

Until Marvel, most comic book publishers believed that only young children read comic books and that most stopped reading them after about three years. However, Marvel's characters, with their everyday problems and complexities, attracted older readers, too. Both teenagers and adults read the books. Across the United States, college students got hooked on Marvel Comics and even formed clubs and reading groups. In fact, one day students from Columbia University in New York City came to the Marvel offices to tell Lee that they had made the Hulk their mascot.

Some colleges even began to offer classes on comic books as a form of modern mythology or folktales. Lee was flooded with invitations to lecture at college campuses all over the United States—something he loved to do. He was thrilled to get such enthusiastic responses to the work that he and the Marvel artists did.

ALL THE RAGE

One of the things that made the Hulk popular with college students in the 1960s was his anger at authority. Lee picked up on the mood of

MORE THAN A SIDEKICK

First introduced as an irresponsible teenager in *The Incredible Hulk* #1, Rick Jones soon developed into a levelheaded, mature person. He became a close friend and protector of both Bruce Banner and the Hulk. Also, during the 1960s, Jones went on to work with the Avengers. He soon became Captain America's sidekick. Later, Jones struck out on his own and became linked to a space warrior known as Captain Marvel. Years later, Jones, in an effort to save Banner, exposed himself to gamma radiation, and for a short period of time he became a Hulk-like creature.

the country. In general, people were angry and frustrated. They mistrusted the government, especially because of the Vietnam War and the response to, or lack of, civil rights. Young people across the country staged protests to show their rage. The Hulk became a symbol for the anger, fear, and frustration felt by young people. The threat of nuclear war continued as well. The Hulk served as a symbol of nuclear, or radioactive, power, as well as a warning about its dangers.

This page from *The Incredible Hulk* #1 shows Bruce Banner in the gamma bomb blast. Kirby's innovative penciling technique is evident. In the fifth panel, he uses thin lines to create the effect of someone caught in a blast without drawing a detailed figure.

In his book *Comic Book Nation* (2002), Bradford W. Wright makes this observation about the Hulk: "His adventures read like an atomic-age western outlaw tale. Roaming the lonely deserts of the Southwest, profoundly alienated from society, the Hulk stood as a creation of Cold War preoccupations and scientific progress gone horribly wrong."

In 1965, *Esquire* magazine asked college students why they liked Marvel comics and who their favorite characters were. Student activists ranked Spider-Man and the Hulk with musician Bob Dylan and Latin American revolutionary leader Che Guevera as revolutionary icons, or symbols.

In 1968, the Hulk became the subject of a song by folksinger Jerry Jeff Walker. The song was called "The Ballad of the Hulk." It was featured on his *Mr. Bojangles* album. In September 1971, the Incredible Hulk, drawn by Herb Trimpe, was featured on the cover of *Rolling Stone* magazine.

5 A GREEN FUTURE

Though the Hulk had a rocky beginning, the character continued to play an important role in the Marvel Universe. In 1971, Marvel teamed the Hulk with Dr. Strange, Sub-Mariner, and the Silver Surfer to form the Defenders. However, his membership in this group was spotty because his antisocial tendencies prevented him from being a part of a team for any prolonged period of time.

THE HULK'S COUSIN

In 1980, Marvel published *The Savage She-Hulk* #1, launching the first direct comic book spin-off of the Hulk. She-Hulk was Bruce Banner's cousin, Jennifer Walters, a lawyer who had been gunned down by a gangster. Thankfully, Banner was nearby and rescued her by giving her a blood transfusion. However, Banner's gamma-tainted

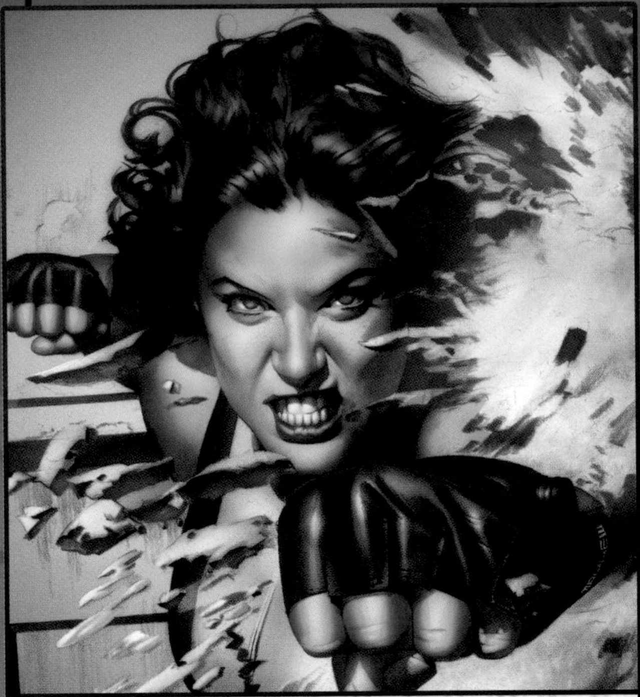

The She-Hulk was co-created by Stan Lee as a way to copyright the idea of a female Hulk for a proposed TV project. The project never happened. Today, She-Hulk stars in her own ongoing series.

blood soon affected his cousin, transforming her into the She-Hulk. She was tall, and green-skinned, and had super-strength. However, unlike the Hulk, she was not a mindless monster—the mind of Jennifer Walters remained in charge of the She-Hulk. She eventually became stuck as the She-Hulk and was not able to turn back into Jennifer Walters.

She-Hulk's first series lasted only twenty-five issues. However, she soon played important roles with both the Fantastic Four and the Avengers. She was a member of both teams, but not at the same time. Over the years, she has starred in several limited series and ongoing series of her own.

THE HULK IN HOLLYWOOD

The Hulk attracted Hollywood producers soon after he was created. He appeared in an animated TV series in the late 1960s. Universal Studios produced a live-action Hulk TV show that aired on CBS from 1978 until 1982. The show starred Bill Bixby as Bruce Banner, and bodybuilder Lou Ferrigno played the Hulk in green body paint and makeup. In the TV show, the Hulk did not speak and was not the product of a gamma bomb experiment. Instead, Banner became the Hulk while doing experiments using gamma radiation that tapped into the strength people had in extreme emergencies.

When the experiment went wrong, it looked like the Hulk had killed Banner. So the Hulk was hunted by the police. Banner, not wanting people to know what he had become, found himself on the run. He always tried to stay one step ahead of the police and Jack McGee, a reporter. Each episode of *The Incredible Hulk* featured Banner coming to a new town trying to find a cure for the Hulk. However, he would always have to become the Hulk in order to save those around him. Besides Banner and the Hulk, no other characters from the comic book appeared in the series.

The Hulk finally reached movie theaters in 2003. *Hulk* was directed by Ang Lee and featured Eric Bana as Bruce Banner. In this movie, the Hulk is completely computer generated. The original

HULK-SPEAK

Through the course of his history, the Incredible Hulk's vocabulary has ranged from grunts and growls to full sentences. Many of his utterings have become familiar phrases. Some of the Hulk's most well-known sayings are "Puny humans!," "Leave Hulk alone!," and "Hulk smash!" However, one of the Hulk's most famous sayings comes from the 1970s live-action TV show. In the first episode, an annoying reporter, Jack McGee, confronts Banner. It is to this reporter that Banner says, "Mr. McGee, don't make me angry. You wouldn't like me when I am angry."

In 2002, Marvel launched a new team book, *The Ultimates*. It was a modern retelling of *The Avengers* and featured new origins for characters such as Iron Man and the Hulk. Marvel's Ultimate Universe Hulk is very different from his regular Marvel Universe counterpart. The Ultimate Hulk does not get stronger when he gets angry. He can only lift about fifty tons.

story was changed yet again. Banner's father, played by Nick Nolte, injects the infant Bruce with a serum that alters his genetic makeup. Then, as an adult, Banner gets caught up in an experiment gone wrong and finds himself turning into the Hulk. Although it received mixed reviews and did not do well at the box office, a sequel is planned that Marvel has promised will be more in line with the comic book character the fans know and love.

SHADES OF GREEN

Today, *The Incredible Hulk* remains one of the most important comic books published by Marvel. It has now been around for over forty years and there are well over 500 issues.

The different versions of the Hulk have been used in alternate Marvel universes. *Hulk 2099* took place in the future. It featured a ruthless businessperson who was exposed to gamma radiation and turned into a Hulk-like creature. He then used his powers to correct the wrongs he previously did. *The Ultimates* is a modernized version of *The Avengers*. In this version of the Marvel Universe, Banner worked on a serum that would turn people into super-soldiers. He became the Hulk when he tested the serum on himself first.

INCREDIBLE FUTURE

The Incredible Hulk remains one of the best-loved comic book characters ever created. He continues to star in his own ongoing series as well as limited series and graphic novels. Bruce Banner's quest to rid himself of the Hulk and live a peaceful life still captivates readers everywhere. And as they have proved in the past, Banner's future adventures promise to be incredible!

TIMELINE: STAN LEE AND JACK KIRBY

1917 Jack Kirby is born on August 28 in New York City.

1922 Stan Lee is born on December 28 in New York City.

1940 Lee goes to work at Martin Goodman's Timely (Marvel) Comics.

1941 Kirby and his partner, Joe Simon, stop working for Timely Comics. Lee becomes the editor and main writer at Timely Comics.

1958 Kirby returns to Marvel Comics and begins working with Lee.

1961 Lee and Kirby co-create the Fantastic Four and launch what has come to be known as the Marvel age of comics.

1962 Lee and Kirby co-create the Incredible Hulk. Lee, along with artist Steve Ditko, co-creates the Amazing Spider-Man.

1970 Kirby leaves Marvel to go to work for DC Comics.

1980s Kirby does the last major comic book of his career for DC Comics.

1994 Kirby dies.

2000 Lee writes a series of books for DC Comics. These books are Lee's versions of Superman, Batman, and Wonder Woman, among others.

2002 Lee starts a new company, POW! Entertainment.

2005 The Kirby family launches the online Jack Kirby Museum.

1962 *The Incredible Hulk* #1: Bruce Banner becomes the Hulk for the first time. The Hulk is colored gray in this issue.

The Incredible Hulk #2: The first appearance of the green Hulk.

1963 *The Fantastic Four* #12: The first meeting between the Fantastic Four and the Incredible Hulk.

1964 *Tales to Astonish* #62: The first appearance of the Leader.

1966 *Tales to Astonish* #80: The first appearance of the Abomination.

1971 *Marvel Feature* #1: The first appearance of the Defenders.

1974 *The Incredible Hulk* #180–181: The first appearance of Wolverine.

1985 *The Incredible Hulk* #312: The revelation that Banner's father physically abused Bruce and his mother.

1986 *The Incredible Hulk* #319: Bruce and Betty get married.

1988 *The Incredible Hulk* #347: First appearance of the Hulk as Mr. Fixit.

GLOSSARY

continuity The consistency within a story or stories as well as an entire fictional universe. Continuity deals with the relationships between hundreds of characters, events, and histories, as well as the past, present, and future of a particular universe.

editor A person responsible for every aspect of a comic, from approving the plot to overseeing assignments, artwork, cover and ad copy, proofreading, production, and printer proofs.

inker An artist who uses black ink to complete a penciller's artwork, readying it for reproduction. The inker brings some of his or her own talent to the page and is also relied upon to make minor corrections.

letterer An artist who uses black india ink and various tools to add words, balloon shapes, sound effects, and panel borders to the page. Today, most lettering is done using computers.

origin The story of how a superhero came to be.

pathos The quality of pity, tenderness, or sorrow that is evoked in an audience of an artistic or literary work.

penciller An artist who tells the story in visual form, determining the page and panel composition that best allows the reader to follow the story. This includes figures, backgrounds, light sources, clothing, and architecture.

plot The synopsis or summary of the story, providing the artist with all the details necessary to illustrate the story.

publisher The person who actually pays the talent, staff, and printer, and determines the look, feel, and consistency of a company's output.

pulp magazine A cheap fiction magazine, usually dedicated to a subject such as science fiction or private detectives. They were called "pulps" because of the newsprint on which they were printed, which was the cheapest kind of paper available for printing. They usually had attention-getting covers, such as people being attacked by space aliens. These were forerunners to the paperback book, and they were hugely successful between the 1920s and 1950s.

script Similar to a movie script, a comic book script breaks a story down into individual pages, describing the action for each panel and what words and captions are required.

word balloon The space devoted to the words spoken by an individual character in a comic story.

writer The person responsible for composing a story given the number of pages assigned. The writer tells the story, in the form of a plot or script, with a clear beginning and ending, providing the visual details and emotions required to effectively communicate to the reader.

Friends of Lulu
13210 Michigan Avenue
Dearborn, MI 48126
E-mail: info@friends-lulu.org.
Web site: http://www.popcultureshock.com/lulu

Museum of Comic and Cartoon Art
594 Broadway, Suite 401
New York, NY 10012
(212) 254-3511
Web site: http://www.moccany.org

WEB SITES

Due to the changing nature of Internet links, the Rosen Publishing Group, Inc., has developed an online list of Web sites related to the subject of this book. This site is updated regularly. Please use the link below to access the list:

http://www.rosenlinks.com/crah/hulk

You can also refer to Marvel's Web site:

http://www.marvel.com

FOR FURTHER READING

David, Peter. *Hulk Visionaries: Peter David.* Volume 1. New York, NY: Marvel Comics, 2005.

David, Peter. *Hulk Visionaries: Peter David.* Volume 2. New York, NY: Marvel Comics, 2005.

David, Peter, et al. *The Incredible Hulk: Beauty and the Behemoth.* New York, NY: Marvel Comics, 1998.

Fingeroth, Danny. *Superman on the Couch.* New York, NY: Continuum, 2004.

Kirby, Jack, et al. *Marvel Visionaries: Jack Kirby.* New York, NY: Marvel Comics, 2004.

Lee, Stan, and Jack Kirby. *Essential Hulk.* Volume 1. New York, NY: Marvel Comics, 1999.

Lee, Stan, et al. *Essential Hulk.* Volume 2. New York, NY: Marvel Comics, 2001.

Lee, Stan, et al. *Essential Hulk.* Volume 3. New York, NY: Marvel Comics, 2005.

Lee, Stan, et al. *Incredible Hulk: Transformations.* New York, NY: Marvel Comics, 1997.

Lee, Stan, et al. *Marvel Visionaries: Stan Lee.* New York, NY: Marvel Comics, 2005.

Leob, Jeph, and Tim Sale. *Hulk: Gray.* New York, NY: Marvel Comics, 2004.

BIBLIOGRAPHY

Blumberg, Arnold T. "Going Green: The Best of the Hulk." *The Overstreet Comic Book Price Guide*, 34th Edition. New York, NY: Random House Information Group, 2004.

Daniels, Les. *Marvel: Five Fabulous Decades of the World's Greatest Comics.* New York, NY: Harry N. Abrams, 1991.

DeFalco, Tom. *Hulk The Ultimate Guide.* New York, NY: DK Publishing, Inc., 2003.

Dorf, Shel, and Rich Rubenfeld. "Interview." *The Jack Kirby Collector*, Volume 10, No. 37, pp. 50–53.

Jones, Gerard, and Will Jacobs. *The Comic Book Heroes.* New York, NY: Crown Publishers, Inc., 1985.

Lee, Stan. *Bring on the Bad Guys.* New York, NY: Fireside, 1976.

Lee, Stan. *Origins of Marvel Comics.* New York, NY: Fireside, 1974.

Lee, Stan, and George Mair. *Excelsior!: The Amazing Life of Stan Lee.* New York, NY: Fireside, 2002.

Raphel, Jordan, and Tom Spurgeon. *Stan Lee and the Rise and Fall of the American Comic Book.* Chicago, IL: Chicago Review Press, Inc., 2003.

Ro, Ronin. *Tales to Astonish.* New York, NY: Bloomsbury, 2004.

Wright, Bradford W. *Comic Book Nation.* Baltimore, MD: The Johns Hopkins University Press, 2001.

INDEX

ABOUT THE AUTHOR

Eric Fein has worked for both Marvel and DC Comics. At Marvel, he edited several Spider-Man comic book series including *Spider-Man, Spectacular Spider-Man*, and *Web of Spider-Man*. He also coedited the first team up of Spider-Man and Batman. At DC Comics, he edited storybooks, coloring and activity books, and how-to-draw books featuring DC Comics Super Heroes such as Superman, Batman, and Wonder Woman. Currently, he is developing and writing several different books and comic book projects.

CREDITS

p. 8 courtesy of the Kirby Estate and *Jack Kirby Collector* magazine (http://www.twomorrows.com) © Kirby Estate; p. 21 © The Everett Collection, Inc.; p. 30 © Frank Trapper/Corbis. All other images provided by Marvel Entertainment, Inc.

Designer: Thomas Forget; Editor: Leigh Ann Cobb;
Photo Researcher: Les Kanturek